The Bus List

Also Available by Keith Dorney

Best Roth! A Beginner's Guide to Roth IRAs, Employer Roth Options, Conversions, and Withdrawals

Maximize Your Earnings With A Health Savings Account

Black and Honolulu Blue

THE BUS LIST

**Essential Estate Planning
Including Wills, Trusts, Durable
Powers, Beneficiary Deeds, TODs and
PODs, Estate Taxes, Plus Organizing
and Securing Your Records**

Keith Dorney

www.keithdorney.com

Disclaimer:

The information contained within this book is not and should not be construed as legal advice. Consult an attorney licensed in your state of residence for legal advice. The information in this book should be considered of a general educational nature. *I publish e-books and print-on-demand books for a reason: I update all my financial planning-related books every year, including this one. I take pride in providing only the most up-to-date information in easy to understand language.* This book will educate you with what is hoped to be correct and up-to-date information, but no warranty or promise is made that everything is 100% accurate.

To Katherine, My love, tireless editor, and inspiration for this book

Acknowledgements

Thanks to Dennis Crandall, Graham Rutherford, Lyndsay Mills, and Darcy McLarty for my teaching opportunities. To the creative Johnny Good: Thanks for lending an ear and the spot-on book title.

A special thanks to Coach Bill Muir.

Table of Contents

Why You Need a Bus List

Hopefully you'll live a long, healthy life and have plenty of time for planning your final arrangements, transferring assets, and fulfilling any last wishes. But what if you get hit by a bus? Even if you don't get hit by a bus, your time will eventually come. It's the one common denominator among all living things.

That's why you need a Bus List. Your Bus List makes it easier on your loved ones during a time of great sorrow and grieving. Compiling your Bus List is one of the kindest, most thoughtful gifts you can bestow on your surviving loved ones. Be sure and make it your last, best gift.

> Through the years, I've learned many folks avoid doing any meaningful estate planning because of brain cramps. That's the term an old coach of mine coined for being so overwhelmed by information you do nothing.
>
> In football, a brain cramp resulted in you standing there looking stupid as the play unfolded around you. With estate planning, a brain cramp could result in consequences much more serious.
>
> Money may be needlessly wasted. Assets could go where you don't want them to go. Your last wishes may not be fulfilled.
>
> The subject of estate planning is broad and at times complicated. The fact that every state has their own set

of rules makes things even more confusing. Then there are those confounded legal terms you have to slog through. It's enough to give anyone a brain cramp.

As I guide you through the process of writing your own Bus List, I'll introduce you to the options available. Some solutions are easy to set up and execute, others are more complicated and costly.

Choose the options that work best for you now. You can always change to a more elaborate plan later.

These decisions and actions on your part ultimately will be wasted if there is poor communication between you and your beneficiaries. Upon your passing, they need look no further than your Bus List. All the needed information is right there in one place.

To help you decide which actions to choose, you'll find a list of "Next Steps" after each section. Complete each applicable next step, execute any necessary documents, and move on to the next section. There are only three sections. You'll have your Bus List written in no time!

After completing all three sections of Part I—Body, Brains, and Bling—you can rest assured you've got the "big stuff" covered.

Section 1 - Body - Detail any last requests, including arrangements.

Section 2 - Brains - Appoint individuals to represent you.

Section 3 - Bling - Assure your most valued assets pass seamlessly and inexpensively to your beneficiaries.

Part II covers other important estate planning topics:

- Location of Your Bus List

- Estate Liquidity

- Federal Estate and Gift Tax

- State Estate, Gift, and Inheritance Tax

- Community Property vs Common Law States

- Should I Hire an Attorney?

As far as confusing legal terms go, I apologize in advance for using some of them, but there is no getting around it.

To help, I've compiled a comprehensive glossary (starting on page 109) of those nasty words, where you'll find easy-to-understand and at times humorous definitions that will add to your breadth of understanding.

> Estate planning is best done when there is no urgency. *If you wait until it is urgent, you've waited too long.*

> Get started on your Bus List now. Don't procrastinate any longer. You can complete the "Body" section in the next few minutes and be one third of the way through!

Part I

Writing Your Bus List

Body

The first item on your Bus List can be a bit difficult to think about, but we've got to have some empathy here. You've just passed unexpectedly. The people who love you are going to be distraught and heartbroken. Plus, they're stuck with you, which of course isn't you anymore.

They've got to decide how to, you know, take care of the body. If you're a Klingon (*It is only an empty shell now. Please treat it as such.*), you can skip this section.

Your Last Arrangements

Do you want to be buried, cremated, dissected, or disassembled? Shall there be a formal funeral and viewing or a more muted affair? What about any religious considerations?

Putting instructions in a will or trust stand the chance of going unread until after it's too late. That's why your last arrangements go at the top of your Bus List.

If you want to be buried, put down here what you have in mind. Fancy a nice plot by the park and the old oak trees, or do you want to be laid to rest back home next to your pre-deceased kin? What about the casket? Do you want a simple pine board model or a fancier one?

If you want to be cremated, note the urn you desire as a receptacle, as well as any other details.

> Personally, I'm insisting my remains be placed in a Folgers® coffee can. Don't make your loved ones guess what you may have wanted, or make them steal an idea from one of their own favorite movies. (Rest in peace, Donny.)

There's a reason this is the first item on your Bus List. In the "Brains" section, you'll appoint a special someone to retrieve your Bus List in the hours after your passing. What they'll need to know right away will be the first thing they read.

Organ and Tissue Donation

Like I'm sure our Klingon friend believed, if someone can use a spare part or two, why not? If you've already signed up, make sure you record your state's registry information or other special instructions in your Bus List.

Besides recording donation information in your Bus List, be sure and talk to your loved ones about it.

> My mom signed up to be a tissue donor but didn't tell anyone. After she died, we didn't find out about it until it was too late and felt terrible we weren't able to fulfill her last wishes.

I've heard dozens of similar stories over the years. If you're serious about your donation, make sure to start your Bus List now and record your donation information along with your instructions regarding last arrangements.

You need to do this even if you're officially registered with your state of residence or other entity.

Most states have forms that make it easy to be an organ/tissue donor. The National Hospice and Palliative Care Association maintain a database of information on your state's programs at www.caringinfo.org:

*http://www.caringinfo.org/i4a/pages/index.cfm?pageid
=32890*

Click on your state of residence to find out what
services they offer.

> I've taken quite a few shots to the head over the years,
> which is why I've pledged my brain and spinal cord to
> the Brain Donation Registry at Boston University's CTE
> Center.
>
> Their research on concussions and links to chronic
> traumatic encephalopathy will hopefully help my fellow
> ballers stricken with the disease.
>
> The folks there assured me if I wanted an open casket
> viewing, that won't be a problem. Apparently they pop
> the top, remove the brain and selected spinal tissue, and
> put you back together pronto. Quite surprising!
>
> I'm officially registered with them as a donor. Just as
> important, my wife and kids know how much my
> donation means to me, and I of course have all the
> details in the Body section of my own Bus List.

Anything you may want to communicate
posthumously goes in the Body section as well. If
you've made a video or other media production,
make sure you reference its location.

If you skip this part of your Bus List, your last wishes may not be fulfilled. You can leave these decisions to someone else, but those closest to you will be grateful you took care of things now.

Picking Up the Tab

During your lifetime, it probably seems you're footing the bill for almost everything. It's no different when you're dead.

That's why it's best to be realistic with those last arrangements. Remember, we're trying to be empathetic. You order up a gold plated casket, live band, and a party for three hundred, those closest to you might just be grieved enough to go for it and then be saddled with credit card debt for the next ten years.

If you and/or your loved ones have the money of Midas, go for it; otherwise, if something grand is planned, make sure your estate has the means to pay for it.

This goes not just your funeral expenses, but for the other expenses your estate will incur when you die. See *Estate Liquidity* (page 80) for more on estate expenses.

Recording Your Decisions

If you've gotten this far but haven't physically started your Bus List yet, strike while the iron is hot! Remember, deciding on a course of action does no good unless it's communicated posthumously.

Before moving on to the next section, where you'll pick "brains" to carry out specific duties on your behalf, choose the form your Bus List will take (if you haven't already).

Here are a few suggestions:

- Handwritten on a piece of paper

- In a notebook stored in your fire proof safe

- On a password protected/encrypted file on your hard drive

- At a secure website in the cloud

Protect your Bus List from identity thieves by taking the appropriate security measures. Get in the habit of storing your Bus List in its chosen location as you write it. Once it's completed, you'll need to update it occasionally so make sure it's convenient yet secure.

See *Location of Your Bus List* (page 77) for more security tips.

Body—Next Steps Checklist

☐ Record details of your last arrangements in your Bus List.

☐ Discuss those last arrangements with the appropriate individuals.

☐ Record any organ and/or tissue donor information in your Bus List.

☐ File the appropriate state or agency-specific paperwork necessary for your organ/tissue donation.

☐ Dedicate appropriate assets to pay for your last arrangements as well as other estate-related expenses.

Brains

Next, it's time to decide who will carry out some very important duties on your behalf. No matter what your situation, age, or level of wealth, you've got to appoint folks to fulfill the following duties:

1. Person who retrieves your Bus List

2. Guardians for minor children (if applicable)

3. Executor

4. Durable power of attorneys for health care and financial management

Person Who Retrieves Your Bus List

The person who retrieves your Bus List must be someone you trust implicitly. In the wrong hands, the information in your Bus List could be used to do you some serious financial damage. Logical choices for this job are one's spouse, trusted offspring, sibling or best friend.

If you are ever declared mentally incompetent, this appointee needs to find and read your Bus List. They'll be in charge of retrieving documents and delivering them to the appointments you'll make later in this section.

Hopefully you won't be declared mentally incompetent during your lifetime (knock on wood). If not, this appointed brain will first read your Bus List upon your passing, and fulfilling your wishes outlined in the Body section would be their first task.

Besides making sure those last arrangements happen, this brain is the keeper of the location of all your assets, including usernames and passwords to your financial accounts, which you'll detail later in the third and final "Bling" section.

That makes where you store your Bus List an important decision. If you haven't started your

Bus List yet, and you're still wondering where you're going to store it, I suggest reading *Location of Your Bus List* (page 77) before going any farther.

Otherwise, it's on to naming more brains. Your Bus List retriever may fill some of your other "Brain" roles, but not necessarily. It's up to you to decide.

Guardian for Minor Children

Skip this section if you don't have kids under the age of 18. If you do, you need a will to name the guardian or guardians for your kids if you get hit by a bus. This is really important. Otherwise, some judge makes the call.

Formalize your decision by drawing a legal will and naming that guardian(s). If for whatever reason your first choice falls out of favor, update your will with an amendment indicating the change. Until your youngest reaches the age of 18, be diligent about monitoring this most important of designations.

Both parents should have the exact same guardian designations in their individual wills to avoid confusion. You might consider naming a successor guardian in case for whatever reason your first choice is incapable of accepting guardianship.

As the Bus List implies, we're talking worst case scenario here: simultaneous death of both parents or death of a surviving parent before a child reaches the age of 18. Nothing is more important than insuring the wellbeing of your kids, so make sure you decide on your guardian pronto and make it legal by indicating your choice in a will.

Brain Cramp Warning: Couples often have trouble agreeing on who is best for the job. Come up with a choice and run with it!

If you can't agree, one extreme compromise is awarding guardianship to your choice if you both get hit by a bus in an even year, and your partner's choice if you get hit by a bus in an odd year. Hopefully it won't come to that.

If you've been taking my advice to heart and you're ready to run off and execute a will to protect your minor kids, be sure and read the next chapter first. You'll want to name your executor or executrix via a will as well.

Executor

Your choice of executor (or executrix if appointee is female) is also named through a will. Although a will can do other things, like bequeathing assets, you need a will if for no other reason than to name your executor (and your guardians for minor kids, if applicable).

Your executor is going to be in charge of things in the months after you die. Duties include:

- Inventorying and appraising assets

- Locating, securing and managing probated property

- filing final tax returns

- communicating with the probate judge and beneficiaries

Your executor may need to hire professionals to properly fulfill their duties. If your named executor isn't local, traveling to and from your county of residence will be necessary.

Your executor will have lots of responsibilities, plus a fiduciary duty (one above and beyond the norm) to fulfill their responsibilities diligently. Ideally, this person is someone you trust implicitly, is comfortable interacting with lawyers and other professionals, and lives locally. Having familiarity with your assets and beneficiaries is also a plus.

If you don't have a will when you die, the probate court, located within the county in which you reside, will appoint an executor for you. A family member may be chosen, but not necessarily, depending on the circumstances.

This administrator, possibly a complete stranger, will need to get up close and personal not only with your stuff but with your beneficiaries as well. Plus, a court-appointed administrator usually ends up costing your estate more money than if you named one yourself.

If you're short on qualified candidates, consider naming co-executors. For instance, your prime candidate might live 3,000 miles away or lack the expertise needed for the job. Pair them with someone who can fill those voids, like a local estate planning attorney or trusted financial professional. Just remember, two people now have to agree before anything gets done, which could complicate things.

Another option is appointing a professional that does this kind of thing for a living. Make sure they have a favorable track record and plan to be in business for a long time to come.

> Oftentimes being an executor is no fun. Dealing with angry beneficiaries, settling disputes between waring family members, and processing bunches of paperwork are often part of the job.

For these reasons please discuss your appointment with your prospective appointee. If they're reluctant to take on the responsibility, you want to know about it now. A named executor has the right to turn down the role when it's game time, so be sure they're willing and able.

You want to consider the possibility you could outlive your named executor, which is why it's best to appoint a backup or two now, even though you can change your choice through an amendment to your will at any time.

This is especially true if you named your spouse as your executor or executrix. Simultaneous death through a catastrophic event is something you don't want to dwell on, but better safe than sorry.

The original draft of your will must be presented to the probate judge to make it legal after you pass. That makes your original will (and any amendments) valuable documents. That's your named executor's first job: Present the will to the probate judge and have it declared legal. Then your named executor can start attending to the rest of their numerous duties.

Greedy wannabe beneficiaries have been known to misrepresent the facts, and that's why the judge wants to see the original will, not a copy. We're talking the one with the dried ink and original notary stamp (required in some states).

You can store your will with your Bus List, but you may want to consider a more secure place. Good choices are your fireproof safe, your attorney's fireproof safe, or a safety deposit box. Indicate its location in your Bus List, and make sure the person who retrieves your Bus List has access.

Speaking of attorneys, you may want to consider hiring one to help you with your will. That way you can be assured it's done right and will be declared legal. See *Should You Hire an Attorney?* (page 107) for more information.

Durable Powers of Attorney

We're almost through with the "Brains" section. Just two more brains to name.

This chapter doesn't have to do with your untimely death. It has to do with losing your mental capacities while you're still alive.

Like most of the subjects we're broaching here, we're talking worst case scenario: You go in for a routine operation and something goes wrong; You're involved in a serious car accident; A form of dementia, like Alzheimer's, Parkinson's or chronic traumatic encephalopathy develops.

If this happens, you won't be able to make your own healthcare decisions or manage your finances. That's why it's a good idea to appoint both a healthcare brain and a financial brain. You may or may not appoint the same person for both jobs: it's up to you to decide.

- *Healthcare Brain* - Given the power to make potentially gritty health care decisions on your behalf.

- *Financial Brain* - Given the power to perform financially related duties like paying bills, depositing checks, filing tax returns, and managing assets.

If you don't make these designations now and you end up in this situation, your loved ones may have to go to court to plead their case as to your medical treatment and to get access to your financial accounts.

> Grant these powers to your brains via a durable power of attorney. A "durable" power means the powers you grant remain in effect now as well as when you're not thinking clearly. A "springing" durable power means no powers are granted until your incapacitation is legally declared.

> Declaring someone legally mentally incapacitated can be a time consuming venture these days with patient confidentiality laws, HIPAA, and the court system, which is why, if possible, to not include a springing power.

> Unless, of course, you are even the tiniest bit afraid the person named might clean you out of house and home or commit other dastardly deeds while you're still alive.

Obviously, granting someone a durable power of attorney without a springing power means you love them and trust them implicitly, because it grants them the right to act on your behalf both now and in the future.

Many states give you the ability to create your own durable power of attorney, plus the means to declare the type and extent of medical care you want administered in an emergency or end of life situation.

These declarations are known by different names, depending on your state of residence:

- living will

- health care directive

- health care proxy

- advanced directive

Be aware that state-specific healthcare directives that do not include a durable power of attorney can't provide for every medical situation and fall short of the powers granted to your appointee through a durable power of attorney. Consider executing a medical durable power of attorney in addition to your state's directive if this is the case.

> Like your other appointed brains, it's best to have a conversation with your healthcare and financial brains now. If your named financial brain is someone other than your healthcare brain, make sure the two brains will be on the same page and able to work together on your behalf.

It's fairly easy to draw up durable power of attorneys that will be legal in your state; however, because circumstances and state laws vary, I recommend doing so through an estate planning attorney who is licensed in your state of residence.

That way you're sure it's done correctly and it's legal. (See *Should I Hire an Attorney* starting on page 107 for a more thorough discussion.)

If you want to do it yourself, the National Hospice and Palliative Care website at *http://www.caringinfo.org/i4a/pages/index.cfm?pageid =3289* is a good place to start to find out what end of life services are offered by your state. Click on your state of residence to download the appropriate instructions and forms.

Another reliable free resource on durable powers of attorney and other legal matters is Nolo Press at *www.nolo.com*.

There are also websites where you can purchase legal services and software. Be sure they are state-specific and from a reliable source if you decide on that route.

Like your will, these original documents should be safeguarded. Note the location of the documents in your Bus List if you're storing them elsewhere.

Brains—Next Steps Checklist

Choose brains to fulfill the following roles:

☐ Person who retrieves your Bus List

☐ Guardian for minor children

☐ Executor (Executrix)

☐ Financial and Healthcare brains

☐ Talk to each brain about their role, and make sure they are willing to accept responsibility.

☐ Visit *www.caringinfo.org*, click on your state of residence and read about offered end-of-life services and download their "Advanced Directive."

☐ Consult with an attorney about drawing up and executing durable powers of attorney and a will.

☐ Record all information from this section, including the location of the original executed documents, in the Brains section of your Bus List.

Bling

This is the section where things can get complicated, but I'm not going to let that happen. The Bus List is meant to be a simple estate planning guide, so we're only going to sweat the big stuff here.

What are your most valuable assets? Those are the ones we need to protect. For most folks, that means retirement accounts, real estate, life insurance, and securities.

Protect from what? We want to protect those high value assets from probate. It's not that your state's probate process is evil; it serves its purpose for those who haven't done their estate planning. But that's not you, is it?

Avoiding Probate

Probate can last a long time and be quite expensive, depending on the size of your estate, circumstances, and state of residence. When property is probated, it is secured, then held and released to your beneficiaries at the end of probate, which on average is years after your death.

Worse, your estate has to pay probate fees on the value of probated assets and any management costs incurred during probate.

That's why you want to keep high value assets out of this state government run process. High valued assets needlessly probated could cost your estate big time and potentially derail your intentions.

I'm not against probate. In fact, you probably want some of your assets probated. Depending on the size of your estate, you'll need cash on hand to pay off debts, pay for funeral expenses, and other estate expenses. Unless you have a trust set up to handle those expenses, this is most easily done through a probated cash account. [See *Estate Liquidity* (page 80) for more details.]

If you've been reading sequentially, you know you need a will to name your executor and guardians for minor children. It is also a convenient tool for bequeathing assets of lesser value and to provide your estate with liquidity in the absence of a trust.

Having high value assets probated, however, could have unforeseen and potentially devastating consequences.

Example 1: High Probate Costs

Colette is an elderly widow with a single daughter Heidi, who works as a schoolteacher. Colette's only remaining substantial asset is her personal residence, market value $650,000. Colette leaves the house to Heidi through her will. Upon Colette's death, the house is probated. Heidi, unable to come up with the money needed to pay her mom's probate fees, watches helplessly as the home she and her family were planning to live in for the rest of their lives is sold to pay the fees.

Are probate fees really that high? It depends on your state of residence's rates, but yes, probate fees can be high, especially on those big ticket items. In the above example, assuming Colette's state of residence was California, Heidi would have had to come up with a minimum of $16,000 to prevent the sale of her mom's house. Some states will charge you more, others less.

Will Substitutes

Feel free to bequeath your beer bottle cap collage, purple-velvet Doc Martin boots, and that coveted Little Pony collection through your will, but do not bequeath a valuable retirement account, life insurance, securities, or personal residence this way. Use a will substitute instead.

Will substitutes pass assets to your beneficiaries upon your death directly without the legal rigmarole and fees associated with probate.

Will substitutes include:

- Beneficiary Designations

- TODs and PODs

- Rights of Survivorship

- Living Trusts

Beneficiary Designations

Beneficiary designations are the easiest and cheapest of the will substitutes to execute. You might have already taken care of this part of your Bus List, but you may not be aware of the power of those beneficiary designations.

When you sign up for your company's retirement plan, take out life insurance, or open an IRA, you sign a contract with that entity for a particular financial service. Included in these contractual arrangements is the ability to appoint beneficiaries via a beneficiary statement.

A beneficiary statement allows you to designate both primary and secondary beneficiaries. If you want to name more than one beneficiary, put names and percentage of inheritance on the primary beneficiary line. The secondary beneficiary declaration is simply a backup in case the primary beneficiary dies before you or refuses the inheritance.

> Don't laugh. In some cases a primary beneficiary might want to refuse an inheritance. Take the case of an affluent elderly surviving spouse. She may want to acquiesce to the secondary beneficiaries, her kids, upon her spouse's death rather than take the inheritance herself.

Make sure all your beneficiary statements are up-to-date and both the primary and secondary lines are filled in. If you're married, your spouse will more than likely be your primary beneficiary. Be sure and name a secondary beneficiary too. That's what your Bus List is all about: Taking care of the big stuff and planning for the unexpected.

What happens if you haven't done your due diligence and the folks you named as beneficiaries are all dead when you pass? You guessed it. Those accounts are needlessly probated.

Accounts that give you the ability to make beneficiary designations include:

- 401(k), 403(b) and 457 Plans

- Simple IRAs, Simple 401ks, and SEPs

- Traditional and Roth IRAs

- Life Insurance

- Annuities

- Some Checking and Savings Accounts (most don't)

Another important fact about beneficiary designations is they *trump any contrary instructions in a will*. The same goes for all will substitutes.

> Check your beneficiary statements now and make sure they are up-to-date and both the primary and secondary designations are completed.

Often your employer, financial entity or custodian in charge of the contract will make beneficiary statements available through their website, along with the ability to edit them.

Make copies and keep them with your Bus List. If you choose to keep your estate planning documents in another secure location, write down the location in the Bling section of your Bus List.

Example 2: Will vs Contract

Sean is a widower with three kids. Years ago, he designated his first born son Luis as the primary beneficiary of his now million dollar 401(k), but later stated in his will he wanted his 401(k) divided equally among his three children. Upon Sean's death, the 401(k) reverts directly to Luis and Luis only, regardless of what the will said.

Even if Luis wanted to share the million with his siblings, as the legal owner he is the one on the hook to pay any taxes; plus, sums given to siblings in excess of $15,000 per year (2018 gift tax exclusion amount) would be considered gifts, complicating matters even more.

TODs and PODs

Another beneficiary designation method is through a TOD (transfer on death) or POD (pay on death). Often called "poor man's trusts" or "Totten trusts," these documents direct to either transfer or pay out assets upon your death directly to the named beneficiary, without going through the probate process.

There is usually little or no cost to set up a TOD or POD.

Use PODs for cash accounts like checking, savings, or money market accounts.

Keep in mind these types of accounts held in taxed advantaged 401(k) type plans and IRAs are protected by beneficiary designations and do not need these protections.

Most states allow you to create PODs on those non-contractual accounts that don't come with the ability to make beneficiary designations. Your financial institution more than likely can provide paperwork and instructions on how to attach a POD to your account that will be legal in your state of residence.

Use TODs to transfer securities, vehicles, even real estate in some states.

TODs for Real Estate

Remember Collette and Heidi's plight? If you recall, Collette transferred her house to Heidi through a will and the house had to be sold to pay the probate fees.

If they resided in a state that allows the transfer of real property through a TOD (also known as a *beneficiary deed*), Collette could have transferred ownership of her house to her daughter through this inexpensive method. They would have avoided probate and those probate expenses, and Heidi would now be enjoying Mom's house as Collette had intended.

You can try drawing up and recording (required in most states) the necessary documents for a legal TOD real estate transfer yourself, but only do so if you have a thorough understanding of everything involved. That's why I advise getting the help of an attorney licensed in your state of residence who is experienced in such matters.

Keep copies of beneficiary statements, TODs, PODs, and beneficiary deeds with your Bus List, or write down where they're located in the Bling section of your Bus List if storing them elsewhere.

Record the web addresses, account numbers, usernames, and passwords of all your accounts too. Update your Bus List whenever any information has changed.

States That Allow TODs for Real Estate

Alaska

Arizona

Arkansas

California

Colorado

District of Columbia

Hawaii

Illinois

Indiana

Kansas

Minnesota

Missouri

Montana

Nebraska

Nevada

New Mexico

North Dakota

Ohio

Oklahoma

Oregon

South Dakota

Texas

Virginia

Washington

West Virginia

Wisconsin

Wyoming

TODs, PODs, beneficiary deeds, and beneficiary designations are an effective method of transferring ownership if you don't want the beneficiary to have access to the account or property while you're alive, or for that matter even be aware of the inheritance prior to your death.

Rights of survivorship is another will substitute that can be used for these types of accounts as well as real estate, but they work quite differently.

Rights of Survivorship and Accounts

Joint tenancy with the rights of survivorship is another will substitute you can use to protect non-contractual property (checking accounts, savings accounts, money market accounts, regular taxable brokerage accounts, etc...) from probate.

Don't let the term "tenancy" fool you. Tenancy and tenants in this context has nothing to do with renting or being a tenant: It refers to joint *ownership*.

You can add a person (tenant) or persons (tenants) to the account before your death. Make sure the joint account includes survivorship rights. Most states will probate regular joint accounts. This gives all parties access to the account.

In end of life situations, it allows a loved one to pay bills and make deposits on behalf of their joint tenant. No gift is made by adding a tenant(s) unless that added tenant withdraws assets for their own purposes. Once the original tenant passes, the account won't be probated, and assets pass to the surviving tenant(s).

Obviously, this could create problems. That other tenant could clean the account out without your consent, or assets could be targeted by your co-tenant's debtors. However, in some situations it's the easiest and best solution.

Rights of Survivorship and Real Estate

Rights of survivorship can also be created with real estate, like your primary residence, secondary residence, land, or income property. By adding a joint tenant(s) with survivorship rights to the property's title, probate can be avoided.

If you're married, a more desirable option may be community property with the rights of survivorship or tenancy by the entirety. It's dependent on your state of residence and whether you live in a community property or non-community property state. [See *Community Property vs Common Law States* (page 97) for more details.]

Deciding how you want to "take title" to real property, or whether you want to change your current ownership designation for estate planning purposes, are important decisions.

Unless you're fully versed in all the ownership options available in your state and clearly understand all the ramifications, it's best to consult with an experienced attorney licensed in your state of residence on these matters.

Example 3: Joint Tenancy with the Rights of Survivorship (Favorable)

Remember Colette and her daughter Heidi from the previous example? If you recall, Heidi watched helplessly as her deceased mother's house, which she bequeathed to Heidi through her will, had to be sold to pay Colette's probate fees. How could this catastrophe have been averted?

Earlier, assuming Colette lived in a state that allows the transfer of real estate through a beneficiary deed (TOD for real estate), we identified one way.

Another way would have been for Colette to change her sole ownership in the property to joint tenancy with the rights of survivorship with Heidi. The property would have avoided probate and passed directly to Heidi upon Colette's death.

By making that ownership change, Collette is gifting half of her house to Heidi, but as long as Collette hadn't made any previous substantial gifts there would be no adverse consequences, tax or otherwise, for Collette's estate. Upon Collette's passing, her half of the house passes directly to Heidi without going through probate.

Property titled with survivorship rights, unlike tenants in common, provide equal and undivided ownership. Regardless of the number of tenants, ownership is equal. Two tenants means each owner owns one-half of the property, three tenants equals one-third ownership each, and six tenants equals one-sixth ownership.

When a tenant passes, their ownership reverts equally to the surviving tenants without going through probate: One-quarter ownership reverts to one-third; One-third to one-half; One-half ownership to sole ownership.

Adding a tenant and creating ownership with survivorship rights during your lifetime is a legitimate will substitute and keeps your property out of probate.

Joint tenancy with the rights of survivorship could have been a great solution for Collette and Heidi, but it can be undesirable in other situations.

Example 4: Joint Tenancy with the Rights of Survivorship (Unfavorable)

Remember widower Sean and his three kids? Let's assume he also owned a $500,000 townhome. Hearing of Collette and Heidi's plight, he goes down to the appropriate government office with the proper paperwork and for a small fee changes his sole ownership to joint tenants with the rights of survivorship with his three kids.

What if Sean wants to move or refinance after making that change? As of the paperwork filing, Sean made a gift of one-fourth of the townhome to each of his three children, so he now owns only one-quarter of the townhome. He'd have to get permission from his three co-owners of the property before making any move. There is also the danger of a lien or other encumbrance being levied against the property if one of Sean's progeny runs into financial trouble.

Upon Sean's death, his one-quarter ownership avoids probate and passes equally to his three kids, giving each of them one-third ownership. What do they do now? Each is one-third owner.

Do all three kids and their families move into Dad's two bedroom townhome and live happily ever after? What if two of the kids want to sell and the other one doesn't?

Even if they all did decide on selling, there could be a big time tax bill lurking because of Sean's estate planning choice.

Gifts and Cost Basis

Another downside to adding joint tenants with the rights of survivorship has to do with capital gains tax and basis if the surviving tenant(s) sell the property. Basis is the original purchase price plus any capital improvements made during ownership.

It's a property's basis that is subtracted from the selling price that determines the amount of capital gains tax owed.

Real property bequeathed through your death, whether through a will or a will substitute, enjoys what is known as "stepped-up basis." This can be of tremendous advantage to your beneficiaries, especially when dealing with highly appreciated assets.

The basis of the property gets stepped-up to the market value of the property at the time of your death, and your beneficiary uses that new basis for tax purposes if they sell the property. With gifts, *the recipient assumes the donor's original basis.*

Example 5: Gifting Highly Appreciated Assets

Let's say all three of Sean's kids agree to sell his townhome after his passing. Because Sean gifted the property (except for his one-fourth ownership) to his kids during his lifetime, they assume his original basis in the property for tax purposes. Only Sean's one-fourth ownership will get stepped-up upon his death: Each kid's basis remains at Sean's original basis.

Let's say Sean paid $80,000 for the townhome twenty years ago and made $20,000 of capital improvements over the years, making his basis $100,000. When Sean made his kids joint tenants, each assumed their part of this original basis, or $25,000 each (100,000/4), as well as assuming one-fourth ownership.

If Sean's kids sold the property, post-Sean, for $500,000, each would owe capital gains tax on a six figure capital gain. Sean could have prevented those tax bills by bequeathing the house to his kids through his will or a will substitute. Then the kids get the stepped-up basis, and assuming the market value of the house didn't change between Sean's death and the sale, no capital gains tax would be owed.

Even though Sean's house would enjoy a stepped-up basis by bequeathing it through his will, it would still have had to go through probate, which as outlined could have its own set of negative consequences.

If there is a single inheritor and the basis of a property isn't much lower than the market price, or the inheritor (like Heidi) has no intention of selling the property during their lifetime, using joint tenancy with the right of survivorship can work. Otherwise, a will substitute like a living trust is often the better alternative.

Living Trusts

I like to call living trusts the Grand Momma of estate planning because they usually offer the best solution for many estate planning objectives. Like other will substitutes, assets transferred upon death through a living trust enjoy a stepped-up basis and protection from probate, but a living trust affords you the ability to literally control those assets from the grave.

> Controlling from the grave sounds a bit ominous and even evil, but it may be prudent for you to do so. Young adults often are careless with large sums of money, for instance. Think of it as protecting your beneficiaries from themselves.

> Plus, you can continue to be a pain in the ass, even after your dead!

There are lots of trusts available for different purposes, but a living trust is the most common type of trust. A living trust is often the only type of trust in an estate plan, or acts as the backbone of a more elaborate plan from which other trusts are created.

> Weigh the costs associated with creating and managing a trust with its effectiveness and convenience.

> The cost for creating an attorney drawn trust starts at around fifteen hundred dollars and goes up from there, depending on its complexity. Additional charges may occur for revisions and management.

Your estate planning objectives may be met by using other less expensive will substitutes.

A Legal Trick

A living trust is nothing more than a legal trick. First, the trust must be created. This is best done through an attorney licensed in your state of residence who is experienced in these matters.

> Although you can try creating your trust from scratch or via software, it is best left to a professional.

> These are complex documents. An experienced estate planning attorney who specializes in trusts will make sure your trust is legal and stays legal.

After you create the trust, property you want controlled by the trust must be legally transferred "into" it. An unfunded living trust does you no good.

You fund it by transferring ownership of property to the trust. After the transfer is made, the grantor or creator of the trust (that's you) technically no longer owns the property; however, since you are in charge of the trust (you name yourself as trustee of the trust during your lifetime), you still enjoy the property as always.

Whatever is owned by the trust stays in the trust and doesn't go through probate when you die. When you create the trust, you decide as to how and when you want the trust property distributed to your beneficiaries per the terms of the trust.

Name Your Successor Trustee

Your named successor trustee (another brain you need to name if you execute a trust) takes over management of the trust property upon your death and is obligated to follow the terms of the trust that you wrote.

Your named successor trustee, like the executor you named in your will, has a fiduciary duty (one above and beyond the norm) to not only uphold the terms of the trust but do what is in the best interest of your named beneficiaries.

Executors and trustees have very similar duties: The difference is your named trustee only controls the property owned by the trust.

With a living trust, you the grantor have complete control. You not only enjoy the property in the trust just as you always had, but you can change the terms of the trust, move property in and out of the trust, change the named beneficiaries, or disband the trust.

See what I mean about a living trust being nothing more than a legal trick? If done right, however, it gives you much more flexibility as to how and when your assets are distributed, while still enjoying protection from probate and stepped-up basis.

Example 6: Personal Residence and a Living Trust

Let's revisit Sean and his three kids. If you recall, Sean added his three kids as joint tenants with the rights of survivorship to his $500,000 townhome. That not only created a bit of a hassle for his kids upon Sean's death, but cost them significant capital gains tax when they eventually sold it.

If Sean had instead created a living trust and transferred ownership of the townhome to the trust with his three kids as equal beneficiaries, upon his death the house not only would have avoided probate, but the kids would also receive the benefit of stepped-up basis.

Upon the sale of the townhome after Sean's death, instead of each kid owing hefty capital gain taxes, tax is avoided entirely [assuming the selling price and appraised market value of the townhome at the time of Sean's death was the same ($500,000 - $500,000 = 0)].

Let's further assume Sean's youngest kid was age 21 at the time of his death, and Sean didn't want her inheriting such a valuable asset at such a young age. Sean could write in the terms of the trust he wants the townhome rented out until his youngest turns age 30.

The terms of Sean's trust could instruct the successor trustee to rent out the townhome. The trust, through the terms of the trust, pays Sean's successor trustee a fee for her trouble. Upon Sean's youngest reaching age 30, the townhome is sold, the proceeds distributed equally to Sean's three kids, and the trust is disbanded.

> The number one reason folks create living trusts is to protect real estate from probate.
>
> If you're married, there is no estate planning issue when the first spouse dies: Their community or joint interest with survivorship rights passes without consequence to the surviving spouse.
>
> It's the surviving spouse who now has an estate planning dilemma.
>
> Just as there is more than one way to bake a cake, there are several different ways you can bequeath assets. It's perfectly fine to go with a simpler, cheaper alternative now, with plans on perfecting your plan later on when you're older and grayer.

Living Trusts and Maintenance Costs

I mentioned earlier that maintaining property in a living trust can be expensive. How expensive? It depends on your attorney.

When moving real estate in and out of a trust, which is necessary when refinancing or selling, legal documents need to be properly filled out and recorded. Unless you're 100% positive you know the correct legal procedures, you'll more than likely enlist the help of your attorney who helped you draw up the trust to help you.

How much will your attorney charge you for those services? During your working years, assuming you refinanced your personal residence three times and bought three homes (and sold the old ones), that's twelve separate transfers that need to be made in and out of the trust.

Folks have reported to me their attorneys only charged a few bucks for these services. Others complained about having to pay much, much more.

Be sure you know what these fees are *before* you decide on which attorney you want to draw up your trust. The above described paper shuffling should only take your attorney a few minutes to complete, but what if they charge $400/hour with a one hour minimum?

Example 7: Using a Will and Then a Trust

Let's once again revisit widower Sean and his three kids. Sean may not want to go to the expense and hassle of creating a living trust when he's young and healthy.

As you now know, if Sean wanted to refinance his townhome or sell it and buy another, laws require him to transfer ownership of the townhome back to himself from the trust, then re-title ownership back to the trust.

This could be cumbersome and expensive for Sean, especially if he plans on moving/refinancing multiple times over the years. On the other hand, he may tolerate the expense and inconvenience for the protection the trust affords (or found an attorney that doesn't charge an arm and a leg for those services).

Another alternative for Sean would be early on to state in his will he wants his three kids to equally inherit his residence. Remember, everyone needs a will, regardless of circumstances or age, to name your executor and guardian for minor children, so this could be done with little or no additional expense.

Once Sean grows older and is more settled, a living trust can then be created and ownership of the townhome transferred to it.

If Sean died unexpectedly (there's that damn bus again!) before creating the living trust, even though the residence would have to go through probate it still goes to his desired beneficiaries.

Once he creates the trust and title to the residence is transferred to it, the trust takes precedence over what was previously instructed in his will, even if he neglected to amend it.

> As in the above example, a will can be used as a "placeholder" for assets, with the intention of eventually transferring them to a living trust.

> That way you're not subject to your state's laws of intestate succession, even though your estate will have to cough up more cash to probate your residence if disaster strikes.

You can transfer just about any type of asset into your living trust. Most assets don't have a legal title like real estate, which makes the transfer less complicated. Simply identifying assets in the terms of the trust is often all that's necessary for the "transfer."

Assets you definitely don't want to transfer into your living trust are your retirement accounts. Tax and a possible early withdrawal penalty are likely.

You could name your living trust as the primary

beneficiary, however. Upon your death, funds transfer to the living trust. The terms of the trust would then dictate how those funds are distributed; otherwise, the assets are transferred directly to your named beneficiary with little or no withdrawal restrictions.

Bling—Next Steps Checklist

☐ Inventory your assets to determine where the majority of your wealth lies. (Those are the assets you want to protect from probate.)

☐ Make a list of all financial accounts and determine which are contracts and covered by beneficiary statements and which are not.

☐ Fill out both the primary and secondary designations for each beneficiary statement and make copies to keep with your other estate planning paperwork.

☐ Decide which of your financial accounts not covered by beneficiary statements or survivorship rights should be probated or transferred via a POD or TOD in the absence of a trust.

☐ Consider protecting your valuable real estate from probate with one of the following will substitutes: living trust, ownership with survivorship rights, or a TOD (if allowed in your state of residence).

☐ Consider a living trust and whether it is right for you now or in the future.

☐ Schedule interviews with three local estate planning attorneys, ask them specific questions (given your new found estate planning knowledge), and pick the best one to help you with your plan.

☐ Record all information from this section, including account numbers, usernames, passwords, and the location of important documents in the Bling section of your Bus List.

Part II

More Estate Planning

Location of Your Bus List

Once you complete your Bus List, you can't just file it away and forget about it. Whenever you change a password, open a new account, or need to swap out a brain or beneficiary, your Bus List needs to be updated. If a major change in your life occurs, like a birth, adoption, death, or job change, that's a good time to read over your Bus List and make any needed changes.

Of course, your Bus List also needs to be assessable by the person you named to retrieve it upon your passing or mental incapacitation. It would be a real shame if you went to the trouble of writing your Bus List and nobody found it until after it was too late.

Don't take your Bus List's location for granted. Most of the items falling under the Body and Brains sections are rather harmless in someone else's hands.

Information in your Bling section, however, is of a highly sensitive nature. Great financial harm could come to you if an unscrupulous individual got their hands on it.

The Bling section of your Bus List more than likely

will contain your social security number, the social security numbers of your loved ones, plus usernames, passwords, and lots of other sensitive stuff. You've got to secure it!

One option is to write down, print out, or save your Bus List and store it in a secure location. Possibilities include an encrypted or password protected file, a file folder stowed away in a secret place, or a thumb drive in your safe.

Another option is to park your Bus List, whether printed out or saved to media, in a safety deposit box. That's probably one of the safest places, but it can be a hassle to have to retrieve it every time you need to make changes.

Make sure your trusted someone has a key and knows where to look when it's game time. If you're rude enough to die on a weekend or holiday, immediate access may not be possible.

There are myriad on-line options too. This is a decision all of us need to make when securing our sensitive data: Do we want to take responsibility for securing it ourselves, or do we turn that responsibility over to someone else?

Share your Bus List's location with one, possibly two or three trusted individuals, depending on your circumstances. In the case of married couples and domestic partners, simultaneous death is rare but can happen. It's just a matter of how paranoid you want to be, but better to err on the safe side.

Keep in mind many identity thieves turn out to be family members. I know this would never happen in your family, but it bears mentioning.

Estate Liquidity

Your estate is going to incur expenses. Make sure you have enough liquid cash available in your estate to pay for them. Typical expenses include:

- funeral related expenses

- probate fees

- executor and administration fees

- debts of the decedent

- state, federal, and estate taxes

- attorney and accountant expenses

If there are insufficient funds made available in one's estate to pay expenses, this could present big problems. That money has to come from somewhere. It can get tricky.

A non-liquid probated asset might need to be sold. Or, if your heirs received assets through will substitutes, your executor and probate judge must decide how to solicit those heirs for their fair share of expenses.

It's like trying to put the Genie back in the bottle, especially if heirs received assets like real property that are not liquid. Often, this can be confusing and makes it extra hard on your executor and beneficiaries.

If you decide on a trust, make sure you transfer enough liquid assets into the trust to handle the job, and specifically spell out their use in the terms of the trust. Another option is to allow the appropriate liquid assets to be probated. Your executor will then have the cash available to pay those last expenses.

Life insurance is another way to provide estate liquidity. Naming your estate or trust as the primary beneficiary insures the amount paid out will be available for use by your named brains.

These expenses are deductible on your estate tax return if your estate needs to file one. If your gross estate is greater than the estate tax exemption amount, you're obligated to file a return, even if you don't end up owing any tax. This goes for both federal and, if appropriate, state estate and gift taxes.

Federal Estate and Gift Taxes

For most, federal estate and gift tax liability is a non-issue because you won't owe any. Thanks to the passage of the Tax Cuts and Jobs Act at the end of 2017, the exemption amounts were raised dramatically. The first $11,400,000 of a decedent's lifetime gifts and estate is not subject to federal estate tax in 2019. If you're married, double it to $22,800,000.

Moving forward, well over 99.9% of estates won't have to pay any federal estate tax. Forget the "one percenters." We're talking the one-tenth of one-percenters! (Not quite as catchy.)

Brain Cramp Warning: If your estate is well under those exemption amounts, do yourself a favor and skip to the next section. The discussion is going to get a bit mind numbing. If your estate's worth is approaching those numbers, take a deep breath and read on.

What's Your Exemption?

If you made gifts in the past of more than the yearly gift tax exclusion amount (currently $15,000 in 2019), your federal estate and gift tax exemption could be less. When gifting more than the gift tax exclusion amount to anyone in a given calendar year, you are required to file a gift tax return to let Uncle Sam know you used some of your gift/estate tax exemption.

To calculate your adjusted exemption amount, subtract the gift tax exclusion from the market value of the gift. Then subtract that amount from the gift/estate tax exemption.

Example 8: Calculating Your Exemption

You gifted $50,000 in 2019 to one of your kids to help them with the down payment on a home. You are required to report a gift of $35,000 (50,000-15,000) to Uncle Sam on the proper form (IRS form 709) and file it along with the rest of your federal tax documents for the year. This reduces your future estate tax exemption by that amount.

It's confusing because even though you have to file a gift tax return, no gift tax is owed until the unified gift and current estate tax limit of $11.40 million (2019) is reached.

You see, Uncle Sam doesn't care whether you give away your assets during your lifetime (via gifts) or through your estate—he's going to get the same tax either way. The gift and estate tax schedules, as well as the gift and estate tax exemption amounts are "unified," and gifts over the yearly exclusion amount erode the estate tax exemption.

Sound complicated? It is, and I've barely scratched the surface. If your estate is approaching or over the exemption, know you've got a bit more work to do, and professional help consummate with the complexity of your situation is warranted.

The value of your gross estate may be more than you think. It is literally everything you own, including the death benefit on life insurance (unless it's in a legal irrevocable life insurance trust-see *Glossary*), the value of all real estate owned, securities, personal possessions, business interests, cash, and any other assets you own. If you're married, also include one-half the value of assets owned jointly or as community property.

Exemption Portability

If you're married, make sure the surviving spouse sees to it that a federal estate tax return is filed on behalf of the deceased spouse's estate.

That way, when the surviving spouse dies, he or she gets to use $22.80 million as their exemption amount rather than $11.40 million (assuming all assets passed to the surviving spouse as is typical with marital estate planning).

Thanks to the American Taxpayer Relief Act of 2012, just two things are necessary to assure portability of the exemption to the surviving spouse:

- Bequeath assets to your surviving spouse

- File a federal estate tax return on behalf of the deceased spouse's estate

Example 9: Exemption Portability Between Spouses

Saumya passes with a gross estate worth $12 million along with $1 million in debts and other expenses. Even though her estate won't owe any tax, her estate is still obligated to file a federal estate tax return because her gross estate was over the exemption amount.

If Saumya is married and she is the first to die, it is especially important that a federal estate tax return is filed, *even if she is under the limit*. That way, her surviving spouse will get to use $22.80 million as his federal estate and gift tax exemption amount (assuming Saumya bequeathed her assets to him as is common with marital estate planning).

As far as federal estate and gift tax planning goes, this simplifies matters immensely. So called AB and ABC estate planning and Bypass Trusts are no longer necessary to preserve the deceased spouse's exemption. If you live in a state that has a state estate and gift tax and a low exemption amount, however, these trusts may still be warranted.

Indexed For Inflation

If the value of your estate is getting up there, making yearly gifts equal to or less than the yearly exclusion amount to one or more folks during the latter part of your life is a nifty way to reduce your estate's worth, thus keeping Uncle Sam out of your pocket. Plus, you get to gaze upon those smiling faces and hopefully see your hard earned money put to good use.

Know that the exclusion and exemption amounts are both indexed for inflation, so you'll be able to make larger gifts in the future, if you so desire, without touching that ever expanding exemption amount.

Year ~ Federal Estate and Gift Tax Exemption ~ Gift Tax Exclusion

2019 ~ $11.40 Million ~ $15,000

2018 ~ $11.20 Million ~ $15,000

2017 ~ $5.49 Million ~ $14,000

2016 ~ $5.45 Million ~ $14,000

2015 ~ $5.43 Million ~ $14,000

2014 ~ $5.34 Million ~ $14,000

2013 ~ $5.25 Million ~ $14,000

2012 ~ $5.12 Million ~ $13,000

2011 ~ $5.00 Million ~ $13,000

With the passage of the Tax Cuts and Jobs Act and doubling of the exemption, only the uber-rich need worry about estate tax.

If you're one of them, remember these numbers will continue to grow. We won't have low inflation forever. That's an important take-away as far as federal estate taxes go. Be generous, and mind the ever-getting-larger gift tax exclusion so you'll be able to take advantage of every penny of your estate tax exemption when it's your time.

State Estate and Gift Tax and Inheritance Tax

State estate and gift taxes, like federal estate and gift taxes, are levied against the gross estate of a decedent. Some state estate and gift tax exemption amounts are tied to the federal amount, which in 2019 is $11.40 million dollars. Most are currently much lower.

Inheritance tax is different than state estate tax. Inheritance taxes are paid by the heir receiving the inheritance, not by the estate of the decedent like with estate tax. Six states currently have an inheritance tax. There is no federal inheritance tax.

How much inheritance tax you pay depends on your relationship with the decedent. Spouses are exempt from inheritance tax in all states. Generally, the more distantly related the beneficiary is from the decedent, the greater the tax rate. These percentages and any exemption amounts vary from state to state.

States have been changing their laws regarding estate and inheritance tax a lot lately. For instance, North Carolina, Ohio, and Tennessee, and most recently Delaware and New Jersey repealed their state estate and gift tax, and Indiana repealed its inheritance tax. Other states, like Rhode Island, Connecticut, Hawaii, and Maryland have raised their exemption amounts.

It's tough to keep track. Check your state of residence's website for the latest changes.

States With An Estate and Gift Tax

Connecticut
https://portal.ct.gov/drs

District of Columbia
https://otr.cfo.dc.gov/

Hawaii
http://tax.hawaii.gov/

Illinois
https://mytax.illinois.gov/_/

Maine
https://www.maine.gov/revenue/

Maryland
https://taxes.marylandtaxes.gov/

Massachusetts
https://www.mass.gov/orgs/massachusetts-department-of-revenue

Minnesota
http://www.revenue.state.mn.us

New York
https://www.tax.ny.gov

Oregon

https://www.oregon.gov/DOR/Pages/index.aspx

Rhode Island

http://www.tax.ri.gov

Vermont

https://tax.vermont.gov/individuals

Washington

https://dor.wa.gov/

States with an Inheritance Tax

Iowa

https://tax.iowa.gov

Kentucky

http://revenue.ky.gov

Maryland

https://taxes.marylandtaxes.gov/

Nebraska

http://www.revenue.nebraska.gov

New Jersey

https://www.state.nj.us/treasury/taxation/

Pennsylvania

https://www.revenue.pa.gov/Pages/default.aspx

Limited State Exemption Portability

States have been slow to adopt portability laws for married couples that sync with the new federal law (American Taxpayer Relief Act of 2012). The estate planning provisions in the American Taxpayer Relief Act make it much easier for a deceased spouse's federal exemption amount to be passed on for use by the surviving spouse, effectively doubling the surviving spouse's available exemption amount (currently $22.40 million for the surviving spouse).

Except for Hawaii residents, there is no such portability of the exemption amount for the widow at the state level, which presents problems for wealthy couples living in states with a state estate and gift tax. Tools like Bypass Trusts, QTIP elections, and AB trust planning may still be useful to reduce state estate and gift tax liability.

Read about those specialty trusts in the *Glossary*, then seek the services of an attorney licensed in your state of residence for help with your estate plan if you're in that situation.

Community Property vs Common Law States

When it comes to estate planning, it helps to be familiar with the laws applicable to your state of residence. This is especially true if you're married. Although laws vary from state to state, how your state of residence handles the issue of who owns what depends largely on whether it is a community property state or a common law state.

The main difference between the two is how the "spousal share" is determined. This is important for estate planning purposes if you're planning a marriage (or contemplating a divorce).

There are ten community property states. If your state of residence isn't on the list, then it's a common law state:

Community Property States:

- *Alaska

- Arizona

- California

- Idaho

- Louisiana

- Nevada

- New Mexico

- Texas

- Washington

- Wisconsin

*Note that Alaska is an "opt-in" community property state, allowing couples to designate specific assets as community property.

Common Law States

Common law states, also known as equitable distribution or non-community property states, handle the concept of the spousal share differently than community property states.

For estate planning purposes, each spouse's share of assets is determined mainly by who is the owner of record. In the absence of a legal title, who the asset was gifted to or who paid for it determines ownership.

Example A: A married man takes title to an automobile in his name only. Common law states assume it was the couple's intent to have the car as his individual asset, so it is considered his sole and separate property, even if both spouses drive it and jointly pay for upkeep.

Example B: A married woman bought a house for herself and husband to live in with money acquired from before their marriage. Title to the house is taken in her name only. The house is considered her sole and separate property.

In a divorce, property is split fairly but not necessarily equally between spouses in common law states. The process of determining each spouse's share is more subjective than in community property states. Factors such as the spouses own levels of acquired wealth, the presence of minor children, the length of the marriage and other factors determine the actual amounts.

In common law states, a spouse cannot exclude the other from an inheritance, even if a deceased spouse had all assets solely in their name. You can't "dis" your spouse through your estate planning.

The forsaken spouse can sue for his or her spousal share and, depending on the circumstances and your common law state's particular rules, be awarded at least half (in some cases much more) of their deceased spouse's estate.

A properly drawn pre-nuptial or nuptial agreement can override your state's rules, as can protecting property through a trust. Consult an attorney licensed in your state of residence for help when drawing up these types of protections.

Community Property States

Community property states handle the concept of the spousal share quite differently than common law states.

Community property states presume all assets acquired during a marriage are owned fifty-fifty between spouses, regardless of what the legal title says or who paid for it. Individual assets owned before a marriage stand the chance of becoming a community asset if commingled with other community property.

Example C: John and Sally are married and reside in a community property state. John makes $400,000 a year. Sally pursues many interests but does not have income. John buys a rustic fishing cabin near his home town in the mountains for his sole and separate use several times a year with friends and family. He takes title to the property in his name only. Even though Sally has never visited the cabin and has no intention of ever doing so in the future, she legally owns one half of it.

Example D: A spouse enters into a marriage as sole owner of a home they both end up occupying after the marriage. Mortgage payments, insurance premiums, and capital improvements are paid for from a joint checking account. Individual ownership of the home eventually reverts to community property where each spouse is a 50-50 owner despite what the title says.

There are three exceptions to the community property rules:

- Property owned before the marriage that is kept separate

- Gifts intended for one spouse

- An inheritance intended for one spouse

Even these assets, if commingled with community assets, can become community property over time.

These community property rules are used for both estate planning purposes and divorce proceedings. Determining each spouse's share of property is less subjective than in common law states. Except for assets attained through one of the three exceptions or an overriding agreement or trust, property is considered owned 50-50 by each spouse.

Community Property with the Rights of Survivorship

When it comes to taking title to real estate, community property states afford an ownership option for spouses not available in common law states. Community property with the rights of survivorship is very similar to joint tenancy with the rights of survivorship with one very important difference.

Joint tenancy with the rights of survivorship, and in some states tenancy by the entirety, are the only undivided ownership options with survivorship rights available to spouses in common law states. When a spouse dies and property is vested with one of these options, only the deceased spouse's half of the property gets stepped-up: The surviving spouse's half retains its original basis.

This could cost the surviving spouse big time capital gains taxes if they decide to sell, especially if it is a highly appreciated asset.

In community property states, assuming title is taken as community property with the rights of survivorship, when the first spouse dies, both spouses half of the property enjoy a stepped-up basis. This can save the surviving spouse a ton in capital gains tax if the asset is sold before their death.

Example E: A couple owns a home with a market value of $1 million dollars as joint tenants with the rights of survivorship. The property was acquired many years before for $80,000.

$20,000 of capital improvements were made over the years. These costs are added to the original purchase price, giving the couple a basis of $100,000. Subtract the basis from the future selling price to determine the capital gain.

When the first spouse dies, only the deceased spouse's half of the property (market value $500,000 with a basis of $50,000) gets stepped-up to $500,000. The surviving spouse's half (market value $500,000 with a basis of $50,000) remains at $50,000.

Let's assume the widow later sells the house for $1.25 million. The surviving spouse won't incur any tax on the deceased spouse's portion of the house, but will incur a hefty capital gains bill on a $450,000 capital gain, despite the home capital gains exclusion of $250,000:

Deceased Spouse's Part

$500,000 minus $500,000 [stepped-up from $50,000 to market value ($500,000) at time of death] equals zero.

Surviving Spouse's Part

$500,000 plus $250,000 of appreciation since spouse's death minus $50,000 basis = $700,000

$700,000 minus $250,000 (home capital gains exclusion amount) = $450,000

If his scenario instead occurred in a community property state, and the couple had taken title to the house as community property with the rights of survivorship, the tax bill would be zero.

No tax is owed since the surviving spouse's half of the property got stepped-up in addition to the deceased spouse's half, and the quarter million dollars of appreciation since the first spouse's death is taken care of by the home capital gains exclusion.

$1.25 million (selling price) minus $1 million (basis) = $250,000

$250,000 minus $250,000 (home capital gains exclusion) = $0

If you live in a community property state and own

your home with your spouse, check the title to see how it is vested. If you can't find a copy of your title, more than likely it's recorded at your county recorder's office and you can get a copy there.

If it is vested as joint tenants with the rights of survivorship instead of community property with the rights of survivorship, consult with an attorney licensed in your state of residence and inquire about changing it.

Deciding how you want to "take title" to real property, or whether you want to change your current ownership designation for estate planning purposes, are important decisions.

Unless you're fully versed in all the ownership options available in your state and clearly understand all the ramifications, it's best to consult with an experienced attorney licensed in your state of residence on these matters.

Should You Hire an Attorney?

I recommend using an attorney licensed in your state of residence to help draw up your will, durable powers of attorney, beneficiary deeds, as well as addressing any concerns as to how to take title to real property. If a trust is in your plans, I doubly recommend using an attorney that specializes in trusts. This insures your documents are legal and done right.

Make sure you interview several candidates for the job, check credentials, and follow up with their references. Discuss the price of drawing the initial document(s) as well as the cost of adding amendments and maintenance of the trust.

If you are unable to ascertain your prospective attorney's approximate fees during this initial interview, consider their vagueness a red flag and move on to the next candidate.

If you're a do-it-yourselfer, there are lots of choices. One option is using estate document-generating software specific to your state of residence that is provided by a reputable vendor.

Type "will maker software" into your favorite web browser and peruse the multitude of choices. Be sure to follow the instructions implicitly, and make sure you answer all questions correctly.

Many states have rules that allow you to execute legal documents from scratch, but your margin for error increases even more. Laws regarding what is legal and what is not vary from state to state, so be extra careful if you take this route.

Remember, if there is any doubt as to an estate planning document's authenticity, it may be declared invalid upon your passing.

Here's wishing you a long, healthy, and happy life.

###

Glossary

AB Trust - An AB Trust is actually two trusts that are used in marital estate planning to utilize the state estate and gift tax exemption amount for the first spouse to die. With few exceptions, AB Trust planning at the federal estate tax level is no longer necessary since the passage of the American Taxpayer Relief Act of 2012, which makes the first spouse to die's exemption portable to the surviving spouse. Except for Hawaii residents, no such portability is afforded for state estate and gift taxes, making AB Trust planning still relevant for wealthy couples. When the first spouse dies, the decedent's living trust or will directs the B trust or Bypass Trust to be funded with assets equal to the state's estate tax exemption amount, with the reminder going to the A Trust or Marital Trust. This arrangement effectively utilizes the state exemption amount of the first spouse to die.

ABC Trust - If you haven't already, read about an AB Trust above. An ABC Trust was utilized for decedents who lived in a state with an estate and gift tax. Before the federal estate tax exemption of the first spouse to die became portable (thanks to the American Taxpayer Relief Act of 2012), ABC Trusts were needed for wealthy couples to utilize both the federal and state exemptions for the first spouse to die. Since the federal exemption became portable, utilizing the state exemption can be accomplished with an AB Trust

Administrator - Term used in some states to describe a court-appointed executor. If you don't name your executor in a will, the probate court appoints one on your behalf.

American Taxpayer Relief Act of 2012 - This comprehensive piece of legislation included provisions making it much easier to preserve the exemption amount of the first spouse to die for the benefit of the surviving spouse. This effectively doubles the surviving spouse's exemption. Two things are required for legal portability of the first spouse to die's exemption: An estate tax return must be filed on behalf of the first spouse to die's estate and assets must be bequeathed to the surviving spouse.

Beneficiary - The recipient of assets. In estate planning it implies the recipient acquired assets through your death. Beneficiaries can be named through wills, trusts, TODs, PODs, and contracts with beneficiary statements.

Beneficiary Deed - A will substitute that allows the transfer of real property without the expense and rigmarole of probate or the potentially high price of a trust. Not available in all states.

Bequeath - To give to someone else through a will or will substitute.

Brain Donation Registry - The Brain Donation Registry at Boston University's School of Medicine accepts donations of brain and spinal tissue from registered individuals who were subjected to repetitive head trauma during their lives in an effort to find out more about chronic traumatic encephalopathy (CTE). Currently, the disease can only be detected and verified postmortem. Visit their website at *https://www.bu.edu/cte/our-research/brain-donation-registry/*.

Bypass Trust - Bypass trusts are used primarily by married couples who live in a state that has a state estate and gift tax to utilize the first spouse to die's state estate and gift tax exemption. Please see AB Trust and ABC Trust here in the glossary for more information on bypass trusts.

Corpus - A legal trust has five elements (grantor, beneficiaries, trustee, terms of the trust, and corpus). The corpus or trust property is what is transferred into the trust by the grantor. It is then legally owned by the trust, not the grantor, and avoids probate upon the grantor's death.

Community Property - A term relative to married couples who live in a community property state. Property acquired during the marriage is considered community property, with 50-50 ownership rights. Property owned separately previous to a marriage can become community property over time unless kept separate, which is best done through a nuptial agreement or trust.

Community Property with the Rights of Survivorship - There is a whole section on this earlier in the book starting on page 103.

Dead - *Synonyms*: answered the call, at room temperature, belly up, bought the farm, bit the dust, chillin', deader than a doornail, expired, extinct, endsville, fettuccini al deado, flatlined, gone fishin', grateful dead, home to stay, Hotel California, joined one's ancestors, kicked the can, knocking on heaven's door, left the building, Morrison hotel, motel deep 6, muerte, out of business, pushing up daisies, rottingham, splitsville, stairway to heaven, street pizza, toe's up, walked the plank, worm farm, zombie playground.

Decedent - A nice way to say any of the above.

Durable Power of Attorney - A power of attorney is a legal document that gives another the power to act on your behalf. The term durable means the power of attorney is valid during your lifetime, even if you are legally declared mentally incompetent. Durable powers of attorney should be drawn for healthcare decisions (healthcare brain) and financial management (financial brain).

Estate and Gift Tax - Tax levied on the estate and lifetime gifts of a decedent at the federal level, state level, or both.

Estate Tax Exemption Equivalent - The estate tax exemption equivalent ($11.20 million in 2018) is the gross amount of a decedent's estate that won't be subject to estate tax. Assuming no estate tax deductions, it is calculated by taking ever increasing amounts of the estate's taxable income to the tax tables, calculating the tax, then subtracting the unified estate tax credit for the year. Think of it this way. If you were to plug in $11.20 million to the Estate and Gift Tax Schedule for 2018, you'd start calculating tax owed first from the 18% bracket, which covers the first $10,000 of the taxable estate. After slogging through the next 11 brackets (ranging from 18% - 40%), adding those amounts together, and then subtracting the unified credit, the answer would be zero. Any amount larger than $11.20 million starts to generate estate tax. Unified means the credit, as well as the estate tax tables, are used to calculate both estate and gift tax. The unified credit, and subsequently the gift and estate tax exemption equivalent, are indexed for inflation and can change year to year.

Executor - A person or persons you appoint to take care of things after you're gone. Name your executor (executrix if female) in a will. Once confirmed, they can act on your behalf after you've passed. Duties include inventorying and appraising assets, securing and managing probated property, communicating with the assigned probate judge and beneficiaries, and filing final income and estate tax returns.

Executrix - Female version of executor.

Fiduciary - One who holds a responsibility to a third party that is above and beyond the norm. Executors and trustees, two brains you may name as you write your Bus List, act as fiduciaries in regard to your beneficiaries. The best interests of the beneficiaries must be paramount when making decisions.

Fiduciary Duty - One that requires due diligence above and beyond the norm. The best interests of the party being represented must be considered and paramount to any decisions made on their behalf.

Financial Brain - This brain, along with your healthcare brain, are in charge of things if you are ever unable to take care of things yourself. You appoint them through properly prepared and executed durable powers of attorney. Your financial brain handles the money end of things, which includes paying bills, making deposits, and managing assets.

Generation-Skipping Transfer Tax - Be aware if you're planning on gifting or bequeathing assets to an unrelated someone who is 37.5 years younger than you, or relatives more than one generation removed (i.e. grandchildren and great-grandchildren), there could be an additional tax owed. The generation-skipping transfer tax has been overhauled by Congress many times the last few decades. The current rendition includes a $3.5 million dollar exemption, so unless you're planning on gifting or bequeathing more than that to your grandchildren, there is no tax.

Gift Tax - See Gift Tax Exclusion and Gift Tax Exemption below.

Gift Tax Exemption - The gift tax exemption (11.20 million in 2018) is the dollar amount of gifts one may give away during one's lifetime that won't be subject to gift tax. Amounts gifted in excess of the gift tax exclusion amount for the year ($15,000 in 2018) counts against this gift tax exemption and must be reported via a gift tax return in the year of the gift. This same gift tax exemption amount carries over and becomes your estate tax exemption when you die. In other words, gifts made over the yearly gift tax exclusion erode both your gift tax and estate tax exemption, which are one in the same. For gifts between spouses, there is an unlimited marital deduction, meaning one spouse can gift an unlimited amount of assets to the other spouse without incurring any federal or state estate or gift tax liability.

Gift Tax Exclusion - The amount ($15,000 in 2018) that can be gifted to an individual in a calendar year without eroding (or owing tax if the exemption is used up) your gift and estate tax exemption (11.20 million in 2018). Amounts gifted in excess of the yearly gift tax exclusion must be reported on a gift tax return (IRS form 709) that is required to be filed along with your other tax paperwork. The gift tax exclusion, as well as the estate tax exemption, are indexed for inflation and can change from year to year.

Grantor - A legal trust has five elements (grantor,

beneficiaries, trustee, terms of the trust, and trust property). The grantor is the person who created the trust for the benefit of the beneficiaries, and who during their lifetime funded the trust with trust property. In a living trust, the grantor typically assumes the additional role of trustee during their lifetime and appoints a successor trustee to take over after that.

Healthcare Brain - This brain, along with your financial brain, are in charge of things if you're ever declared mentally incompetent. You appoint them through properly prepared and executed durable power of attorneys. This enables your healthcare brain to make healthcare decisions on your behalf when you are not able.

HIPAA - Acronym for the Health Insurance Portability and Accountability Act of 1996. This sweeping legislation better protects the security of your health information, whether written, electronic, or orally communicated. It also protects individual rights to health insurance in regard to pre-existing conditions and those seeking continued coverage.

Home Capital Gains Exclusion - My favorite piece of legislation ever! It allows a taxpayer to exclude the first $250,000 of capital gain on the sale of their personal residence. Married taxpayers get to exclude double that amount, or $500,000. The law states in order to qualify, the dwelling had to be lived in as your personal residence for two out of the last five years. There are no age restrictions (other than being old enough to own real property), and a taxpayer can take advantage of the exclusion multiple times during their lifetime.

Inheritance Tax - Some states charge the beneficiary an inheritance tax (page 95) when they receive assets from an estate. This is unlike an estate tax where the estate pays the taxes, not the beneficiary. Some beneficiaries, dependent on their relationship with the deceased, are exempt from paying inheritance tax.

Intestate Succession (Laws of) - Who gets what when you pass if you've failed to do any estate planning? That's up to the laws of intestate succession that your state of residence has written. If you die "intestate," assets are first probated and then distributed according to this list. The first person on that list may be the last person you want to get your stuff, so it's best for you to decide now.

Irrevocable Life Insurance Trust - This is a sneaky way to avoid having the face amount of a life insurance policy included in your gross estate when you pass. A trust is created, and typically the grantor transfers an unfunded life insurance policy to it. The grantor pays the insurance premiums through gifts to the trust. These gifts are at or under the year's gift tax exclusion amount. The sneaky part lies in creating a "present interest" for those gifts. Letters are written to the beneficiaries of the trust acknowledging the gifts, giving them the opportunity to collect their gift during a specific time period. If done correctly, upon the grantor's death, the insurance payout to the named beneficiary is not included in the grantor's estate. As the name implies, this is an irrevocable trust and the elements of the trust cannot be changed by the grantor once it is created.

IRS Form 709 – File this form to report gifts that are subject to gift tax or generation-skipping transfer tax. You probably won't have to pay any tax until if and when you use up your estate and gift tax exemption of 11.20 million. That's above and beyond the year's current gift tax exclusion.

Living Trust - A revocable trust that can be used as a will substitute. There is a whole section on living trusts in this book (page 63).

Marital Assets - Assets acquired during one's marriage with their spouse. In community property states, assets acquired during a marriage are considered marital assets regardless of which spouse paid for them or how it is titled, unless the property falls under one of the three exceptions: Property owned before the marriage that is kept separate; Gifts intended for one spouse; An inheritance intended for one spouse.

Mentally Incompetent - Whether because of an accident, an incident during surgery or through an end of life situation, there may be a time before your death when you are unable to make your own healthcare decisions or manage your finances. That's why it's smart to execute durable powers of attorneys and name individual(s) to act upon your behalf for these purposes if this ever happens. These days, it can be time consuming to legally have someone declared mentally incompetent, which is important when it comes to whether you want to include a "springing power" in the above referenced documents.

POD - Often referred to as a Totten Trust, Poor Man's Trust, or **Pay-On-Death**. This designation grants the ability to transfer cash upon your death from a checking, savings, money market, or other cash account to a named beneficiary. PODs and TODs are valid will substitutes and assets avoid the probate process. After legal necessities are completed, including issuance of a death certificate, money is transferred directly to the named beneficiary without going through the probate process.

Power of Attorney - A legal document giving another the right to act on your behalf. It can be specific to a particular instance and time, or it can be more general. In estate planning, durable power of attorneys should be drawn for two purposes: healthcare decisions and financial management. "Durable" means that the powers granted are still valid if you are declared mentally incompetent. (A power of attorney without a durable moniker is not valid if you are declared mentally incompetent.) You may or may not want to add a "springing power" to your durable power of attorneys.

Present Interest - The yearly gift tax exclusion can only be used if the person receiving the gift has an immediate right to it. For example, if I put $15,000 in an irrevocable trust for you, but the terms of the trust say you can't have it until I die, that's not a present interest and I'd be required to file a gift tax return to report that $15,000 gift. It is important to create a present interest when making gifts to an irrevocable life insurance trust (page 118), for example.

Primary Beneficiary - Contracts for life insurance, IRAs, 401(k) type plans, annuities, stock awards, employee stock purchase plans and more give you the ability to name a primary as well as a secondary beneficiary. These designations are valid will substitutes, meaning assets pass directly to the beneficiary without going through the probate process. Naming someone a primary beneficiary overrides any contradictory information that may be contained in a will. Remember that the secondary beneficiary designation is there just as a backup if the primary beneficiary pre-deceases you or refuses the inheritance. If you want to split an inheritance, put all recipients as primary beneficiaries with the appropriate percentages.

Primary Residence - It's the place that you call home. If you own both a primary and secondary residence, it's the one where you spend the majority of your time. In most cases, the state where your primary residence is located determines your state of residence for tax purposes.

Probate - A legal process run by your state of residence to help close out a decedent's last affairs, including distributing assets to heirs. Property bequeathed through a will is held, managed, and distributed through the probate process, as is property not named through a valid will substitute.

Probate Court - A specialized court run by your state of residence. Besides administering a decedent's estate, probate court also has jurisdiction over matters of conservancy and guardianship.

QTIP Election – This election gives the executor of an estate the option of either taking advantage of the unlimited marital deduction and passing on the value or a portion of the value of a QTIP Trust to the surviving spouse or including the value or a portion of the value of the estate in the decedent's estate. This flexibility can be important when trying to minimize estate taxes for both spouses. Besides limiting the surviving spouse's access to the corpus of the trust and disallowing changes as to the eventual beneficiaries of the trust, a QTIP Trust and potential QTIP Election can be an important tool to help minimize the estate taxes paid by a couple.

QTIP Trust - Stands for qualified terminal interest property trust. This trust is often used in estate planning to protect one's assets acquired prior to a marriage from becoming a marital asset. A life estate is created for the benefit of a beneficiary from assets transferred to the trust upon death of the grantor. This beneficiary, often the spouse the divorced grantor married after a prior marriage with kids, enjoys the assets during their lifetime. Upon the passing of this beneficiary, property in the trust reverts to other named beneficiaries, often the first spouse to die's children from a previous marriage. QTIP trusts are also used in state estate and gift tax planning to maximize each spouse's state estate and gift tax exemption, as well as to help minimize generation-skipping transfer taxes.

Real Property - For our purposes we are talking your personal residence, secondary residence, land, income property and other interests in real estate you own. Protecting real property from probate is a primary reason for creating living trusts.

Rights of Survivorship - A designation for accounts and real estate that acts as a will substitute. Upon the death of an owner or "tenant," their share of assets passes equally to the surviving tenant or tenants without going through probate.

Secondary Beneficiary - Contracts for life insurance, IRAs, 401(k) type plans, annuities, stock awards, employee stock purchase plans and more come with not only the ability to name a primary beneficiary but a secondary one as well. It gives you a "backup" in case your primary beneficiary pre-decease's you. Your Bus List includes planning for the unexpected, so be sure both your primary and secondary beneficiary designations are filled out on all accounts that come with beneficiary statements, and keep them updated.

Springing Power - A durable power of attorney may contain this power, which means it only becomes valid or "springs" into action upon occurrence of an event, in this case if you are ever declared mentally incompetent. Spouses who trust and love each other usually don't include a springing power when naming their spouse as their durable power of attorney since having one declared legally incompetent can be a time consuming process.

Stepped-Up Basis – Assets passed along to beneficiaries through one's estate, i.e. through your death, enjoy what's known as stepped-up basis. With gifts made during your lifetime, the one receiving the gift assumes the person giving the gift's original basis. Basis is simply what was paid for the asset, plus any capital improvements (if applicable). It's what is subtracted from the sale price of an asset to determine capital gains tax.

When assets are bequeathed through your death, the asset's basis gets "stepped-up" to the market value of the asset at the time of your death. This is especially important with highly appreciated assets. Large amounts of capital gains liability can get "wiped away" through such an after-death transfer.

Successor Trustee - A person named in a trust that takes over management of the trust once the original trustee no longer can serve because of death, withdrawal, or dismissal. In a living trust the successor trustee, in most cases, assumes duties after the grantor's death. (A typical living trust arrangement has the grantor of the trust also acting as the trustee of the trust during their lifetime.) The successor trustee is bound to act by the terms of the trust (written by the grantor) and has a fiduciary duty in regards to the beneficiaries.

Survivorship Rights - A designation for accounts and real estate that acts as a will substitute. Upon the death of an owner or "tenant," their share of assets passes equally to the surviving tenant or tenants without going through probate.

Tax Cuts and Jobs Act - Signed into law by President Trump on December 22, 2017, this legislation dramatically changed the taxation landscape for 2018 and beyond. For businesses, corporate taxes were slashed to a flat 21%, a new 20% deduction in taxable income for "pass through businesses," and the alternative minimum tax was repealed. These tax changes are permanent (or until Congress decides to change them again) and have no sunset. Personal taxes were lowered substantially too, but these changes expire (sunset) at the end of 2025 and include the following: Seven new tax brackets of 10%, 12%, 22%, 24%, 32%, 35%, and 37% to determine taxable income along with more tax-friendly thresholds; Stricter limits on deductibility of state and local income taxes and mortgage interest; The repeal of deductions for personal exemptions and miscellaneous itemized deductions; The nearly doubling of the standard deduction and an expanded child tax credit; A crackdown on the Kiddie Tax and a more tax-friendly AMT calculation; Expanded limits on federal gift and estate tax.

Tenancy by the Entirety - This form of ownership is for married couples only, and is not available in all states. Generally, community property states offer community property with the rights of survivorship ownership and common law states tenancy by the entirety ownership. It affords the same advantages as joint tenancy with the rights of survivorship, including survivorship rights and undivided ownership, but may offer greater protection from the debts of a spouse.

Tenant - When used in estate planning, a tenant does not refer to a landlord-tenant relationship. Rather, it refers to owners of real property. In a joint tenancy with the rights of survivorship vesting, each tenant or owner has undivided equal ownership, and when one tenant passes, their share goes equally to the surviving tenants.

Tenants in Common - Unlike joint tenancy with rights of survivorship, where ownership is equal and a decedent's share passes to the surviving tenants equally, tenants in common is divided ownership without survivorship rights. Ownership can be unequal and of any percentage, and ownership can be sold or passed on to heirs without restriction or permission from other tenants (assuming no partnership agreement is in place that says otherwise).

Terms of the Trust - A legal trust has five elements (grantor, beneficiaries, trustee, terms of the trust, and trust property). The terms of the trust act as instructions as to how assets in the trust are managed and distributed. In an irrevocable trust, the terms cannot be altered. In a revocable trust the terms of the trust, as well as the other elements of the trust, may be changed during the grantor's lifetime. Once the grantor of a living trust passes, the trust typically becomes irrevocable and the successor trustee is bound by the terms of the trust.

Testamentary Trust - One of the main functions of trusts is to avoid the probate process by transferring assets to a trust during your lifetime. A Testamentary Trust is an exception to that rule: It is created through a will and is funded through probate and is a part of the probate process. Testamentary Trusts are often created to plan for an event that is unlikely to happen, like the death of a single parent or simultaneous death of both parents before a child reaches the age of 18. Designated assets are transferred into the Testamentary Trust. You name a trustee who is in charge of managing those assets. Assets bequeathed to children can be managed until they reach the age of majority or a later date if you so desire. You designate that date through the terms of the trust. Make sure you also designate guardian(s) for your minor children via your will.

TOD - Stands for **Transfer-on-Death**. Similar to a POD except it affords assets rather than cash to be transferred to a named beneficiary upon the death of a decedent. Use TODs to avoid probate and transfer assets like stocks, bonds, and even real estate in some states. TODs for real estate are often referred to as beneficiary deeds.

Totten Trust - A Totten Trust is simply another name for a POD (Pay-On- Death), so see POD here in the glossary for a definition. The name dates from a 1904 court decision that first created this valid will substitute.

Trust - A trust is a document that creates a separate legal entity. Assets transferred into the trust by the grantor become the property of the trust, not the grantor. There are many different types of trusts used for myriad reasons. Trusts can be revocable or irrevocable.

Trust Property - A legal trust has five elements (grantor, beneficiaries, trustee, terms of the trust, and trust property). The trust property or corpus is what is transferred into the trust by the grantor. It is then legally owned by the trust, not the grantor, and avoids probate upon the grantor's death.

Unified Credit - The unified credit is used for calculating both estate and gift tax liability. Unified refers to the fact that the estate and gift tax schedules are one in the same. You see, Uncle Sam doesn't care whether you gift your assets during your lifetime or through your death: He gets the same tax either way. Making gifts over the gift tax exclusion amount for the year erodes your unified gift and estate tax exemption. No tax is due until the exemption amount is reached (currently $11.20 million in 2018). Whether that occurs before your death via extraordinary gift giving or after via your estate, Uncle Sam still receives the same tax.

Will – Most folks think of a will's main function as designating who gets what when you die. Using a will in this manner is fine for items of lesser value, but for your most valuable of assets use a Will Substitute (page 44) instead. Assets passed along by your will are subject to probate, which may be time consuming and expensive for your named beneficiaries. You'll still need a will, however, to name your executor or executrix, designate guardian(s) for minor children, set up a Testamentary Trust, as well as other functions.

Will Substitute - Refers to TODs, PODs, beneficiary deeds, trusts, beneficiary designations, rights of survivorship, and other legal designations where assets are transferred directly to beneficiaries rather than through the probate process.

About Keith Dorney

Thank you for reading my book on essential estate planning. Once you've written your own Bus List and have the big stuff covered, you sleep a bit easier at night.

I'd appreciate it if you could take a moment to leave a review. Visiting *www.thebuslist.com* will take you to the book's sales page at Amazon, then click on "customer reviews" to leave feedback. Thanks!

You might be interested in another financial planning-related topic that I'm passionate about: Employer-offered Roth options and Roth IRAs. Why do I get so excited about these accounts? The tax advantages potentially make them the top performers in your arsenal of retirement savings vehicles.

The trick is to know when and how to invest in them. Money socked away now in Roth accounts will probably have a bigger bang for the buck than Roth money invested later. Tax-free earnings compound into big tax-free numbers the longer they have to percolate.

It can get complicated, trying to decide not only

what type of contributions to make, but how to invest those contributions.

Best Roth! A Beginner's Guide to Roth IRAs, Employer Roth Options, Conversions, and Withdrawals can help. It explains your options and helps you formulate your own investment plan for both now and in the future.

Typing "best roth" into search at Amazon.com will take you to the sales page. Thanks for checking it out!

I'm proud of my accomplishments as a financial author and teacher, but you may know me better as a former football player. Check out all my books at www.KeithDorney.com.

After moving on from the NFL and the Detroit Lions, my wife Katherine and I settled in Sonoma County, California, where we raised our two kids and still reside. Besides teaching and writing, I enjoy hanging out in the garden and spending time with family and friends.

Made in the USA
Middletown, DE
10 May 2019